GRANDMA MARGIE'S TALE OF THE 123'S OF THE BIBLE: TRUE OR FALSE

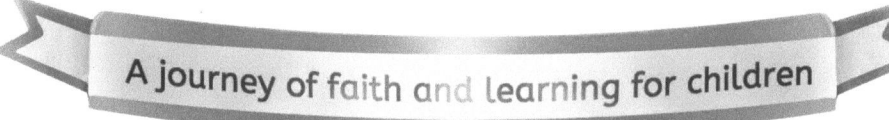

A journey of faith and learning for children

Written by **Dr. K.T. Zulkowski**

Published by Mz. Kim Productions

4263 Tierra Rejada Rd #151

Moorpark, CA 93021

www.mzkimproductions.com

ISBN: 978-1-962106-18-4

Printed in United States of America

First Printing: September 2023

Date of Copyright: July 5,2023

For permissions, please contact: Mz. Kim Productions

4263 Tierra Rejada Rd #151

Moorpark, CA 93021

www.mzkimproductions.com

mzkimproductions@gmail.com

Dedication

This book is lovingly dedicated to all the grandmothers around the world, who, with their wisdom, love, and faith, guide us on our journey through life. Your stories and lessons are the threads that weave the fabric of our lives.

To my own grandmother, whose spirit lives on in the pages of this book, thank you for teaching me the 1 2 3's of life and faith.

And finally, to all the young readers, may this book inspire you to explore the beautiful teachings of the Bible and fill your hearts with love, joy, and faith. Remember, every story is a stepping stone on the path of learning and every number is a key to unlock the doors of wisdom.

Happy reading!

Dr. K.T. Zulkowski

Educational Value

"Grandma Margie's Tale of the 123's of the Bible: True or False " holds immense educational value for children. It introduces young readers to key biblical stories and characters, fostering an early understanding of Christian faith and values. The use of numbers as a teaching tool aids in the development of numerical literacy, making the book a great resource for early math learning. The book also encourages reading skills and vocabulary expansion, as children are introduced to new words and concepts. The engaging dialogue and questions posed by the characters promote critical thinking and comprehension skills. Furthermore, the book's themes of love, faith, friendship, and servanthood provide valuable moral lessons. The illustrations also add an artistic element, helping children to visualize the stories and enhancing their imaginative skills. Overall, this book is a comprehensive educational tool, combining religious education, literacy development, moral lessons, and artistic appreciation.

In addition to the aforementioned educational values, " Grandma Margie's Tale of the 1,2,3's of the Bible: True or False " also introduces children to the concept of storytelling. The narrative structure of the book, with its progression from one biblical event to another, helps children understand how stories are constructed and sequenced. This can enhance their narrative skills and their ability to comprehend and create stories of their own.

The book also encourages interactive learning. The dialogue between Grandma Margie and her grandchildren invites readers to participate in the discussion, fostering active engagement with the text. This can enhance children's listening and speaking skills, as well as their ability to engage in meaningful discussions.

Moreover, the book promotes cultural and historical awareness. By introducing children to biblical stories, it provides them with insights into the historical and cultural contexts of these narratives. This can broaden their understanding of the world and its diverse cultures and histories.

The book's emphasis on values such as love, faith, and servanthood also contributes to character education. It encourages children to reflect on these values and how they can apply them in their own lives, fostering personal growth and ethical development.

Lastly, the book can also enhance children's visual literacy. The illustrations not only support the text but also tell a story of their own. By interpreting these images, children can develop their ability to understand visual information, which is a crucial skill in today's image-saturated world.

Zipporah and Zion: Yes, Grandma Margie!

Grandma Margie: **1** is for One God. The Bible tells us in Deuteronomy 6:4, "Hear, O Israel: The Lord our God, the Lord is one." God is the creator of everything and loves us all.

Zion: Grandma, what are the Two Tablets?

Grandma Margie: **2** is for Two Tablets. In Exodus 31:18, God gave Moses two stone tablets with the Ten Commandments written on them. They teach us how to live a life that pleases God and shows love to others.

Zipporah: Grandma, who are the Three Wise Men?

Grandma Margie: **3** is for Three Wise Men. In Matthew 2:1-2, wise men from the East followed a star to find baby Jesus and brought Him gifts. They teach us about seeking and worshiping Jesus with all our hearts.

Zion: Grandma, who are the Four Friends?

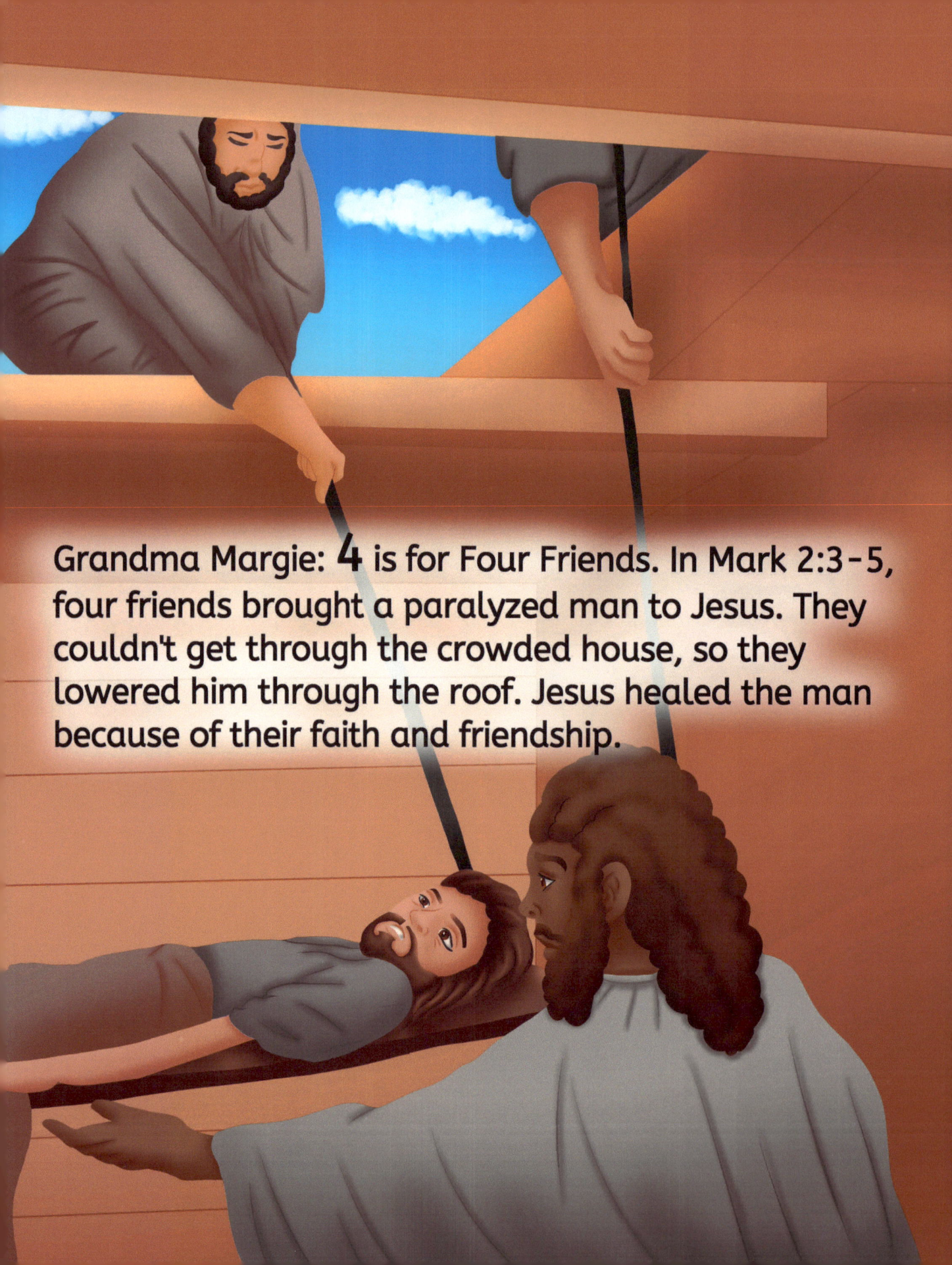

Grandma Margie: **4** is for Four Friends. In Mark 2:3-5, four friends brought a paralyzed man to Jesus. They couldn't get through the crowded house, so they lowered him through the roof. Jesus healed the man because of their faith and friendship.

Zipporah: Grandma, what are the Five Loaves and Two Fish?

Grandma Margie: **5** is for Five Loaves and Two Fish. In Matthew 14:17-21, Jesus fed a crowd of five thousand people with only five loaves of bread.

Grandma Margie: **6** is for Six Disciples. In John 13:4-5, Jesus humbly washed the feet of his disciples to teach them about servanthood and love for one another.

Zion: Grandma, what happened on the Seventh Day?

Grandma Margie: **7** is for Seven Days of Creation. In Genesis 1, God created the world in six days and rested on the seventh day, setting it apart as a holy day of rest.

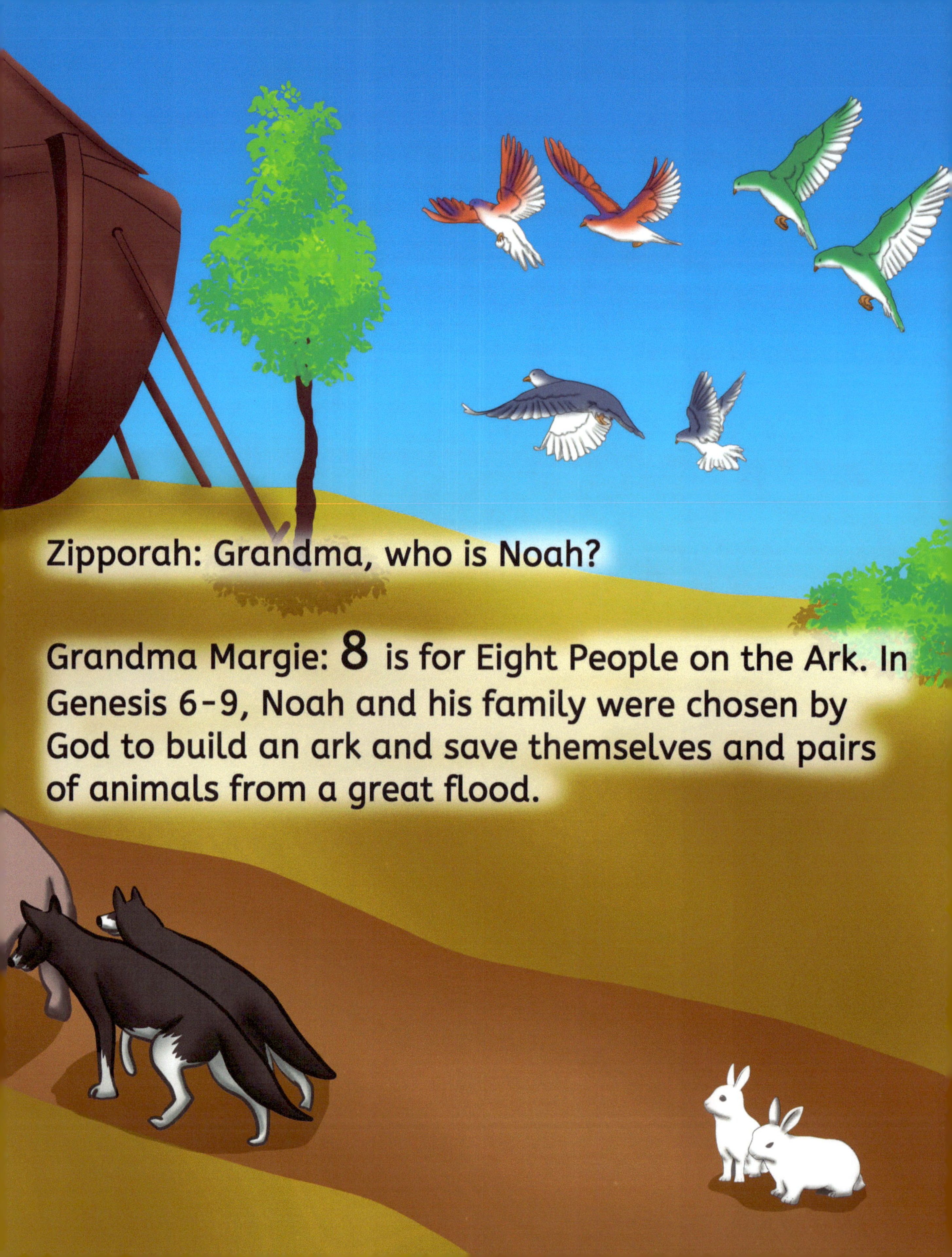

Zipporah: Grandma, who is Noah?

Grandma Margie: **8** is for Eight People on the Ark. In Genesis 6-9, Noah and his family were chosen by God to build an ark and save themselves and pairs of animals from a great flood.

Grandma Margie: **9** is for Nine Fruits of the Spirit. In Galatians 5:22-23, the Bible tells us that the Holy Spirit produces love, joy, peace, patience, kindness, goodness, faithfulness, gentleness, and self-control in our lives.

Zion: Grandma, what do the Ten Commandments teach us?

You shall have no other gods before me.

You shall not take the name of the Lord your God in vain.

Remember that you keep holy the sabbath day.

Honour your father and your mother.

You shall not kill.

Grandma Margie: **10** is for Ten Commandments. In Exodus 20, God gave us these commandments to guide us in living a life that honors Him and respects others.

You shall not commit adultery.

You shall not steal.

You shall not bear false witness against your neighbor.

You shall not covet your neighbor's wife.

You shall not covet your neighbor's goods.

Zipporah: Grandma, why is there an empty chair?

Grandma Margie: **11** is for Eleven Faithful Disciples. After Judas betrayed Jesus, there were eleven remaining disciples who continued to follow and spread His teachings.

Grandma Margie: **12** is for Twelve Apostles. Jesus chose twelve disciples to be His closest followers and to carry on His mission after He returned to heaven.

Grandma Margie: **13** is for Thirteen Tribes of Israel. After the twelve sons of Jacob, also known as the twelve tribes of Israel, Joseph's two sons, Ephraim and Manasseh, each became tribes, making a total of thirteen tribes.

Zion: Grandma, why was Samson so strong?

Grandma Margie: **14** is for Fourteen Days of Samson's Riddle. In Judges 14, Samson posed a riddle to his wedding guests and gave them fourteen days to solve it. It was a test of their wisdom and determination. Samson's strength was a result of a divine blessing. It was said that he was given supernatural power by God, which enabled him to perform amazing feats of strength, such as tearing apart a lion Samson's strength served as a symbol of his unique purpose and role in God's plan for his life.

Zipporah: Grandma, why did people start speaking different languages?

Grandma Margie: **15** is for Fifteen Different Languages. In Genesis 11, the people of Babel tried to build a tower to reach the heavens. As a result, God confused their languages, making communication difficult.

Grandma Margie: **16** is for Sixteen Years of Joseph's Life in Egypt. After being sold into slavery by his brothers, Joseph became a powerful leader in Egypt and eventually reunited with his family.

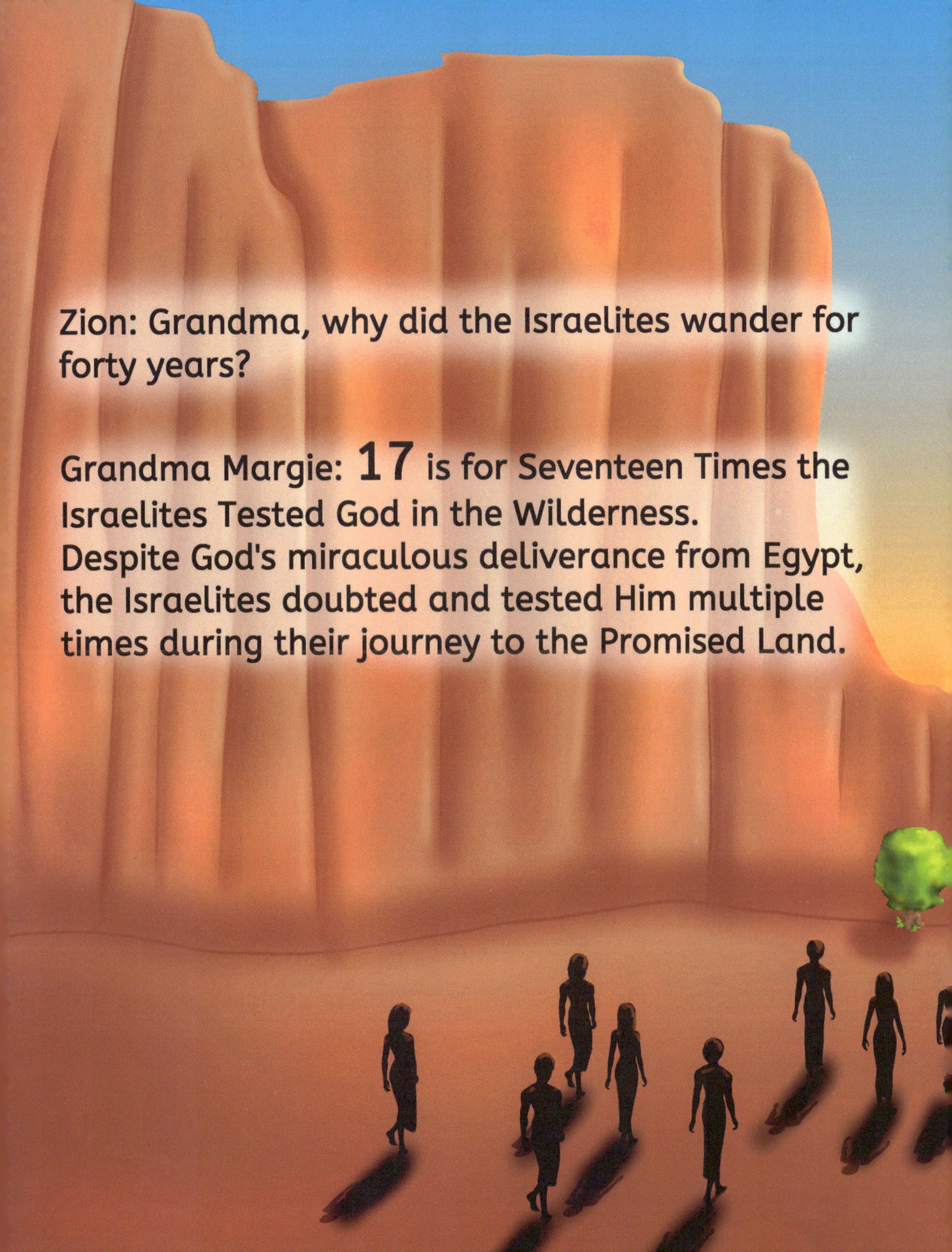

Zion: Grandma, why did the Israelites wander for forty years?

Grandma Margie: **17** is for Seventeen Times the Israelites Tested God in the Wilderness.
Despite God's miraculous deliverance from Egypt, the Israelites doubted and tested Him multiple times during their journey to the Promised Land.

Zipporah: Grandma, did the lions hurt Daniel?

Grandma Margie: **18** is for Eighteen Nights Daniel Spent in the Lion's Den. In Daniel 6, Daniel's faithfulness to God led to him being thrown into a den of lions. But God protected him, and he emerged unharmed.

Grandma Margie: **19** is for Nineteen Years of Esther's Preparation to Become Queen. In the book of Esther, Esther went through a long process of beauty treatments and training before she became queen and saved her people.

Zion: Grandma, how long was Jonah inside the fish?

Grandma Margie: **20** is for Twenty Days and Nights Jonah Spent in the Belly of the Fish. Jonah was swallowed by a big fish after trying to run away from God's command, and he stayed inside it for three days and three nights.

Zipporah: Grandma, how did Jesus feed so many people?

Grandma Margie: **21** is for Twenty-One Baskets of Leftover Food. In Matthew 14, Jesus miraculously fed five thousand people with only five loaves of bread and two fish, and they.

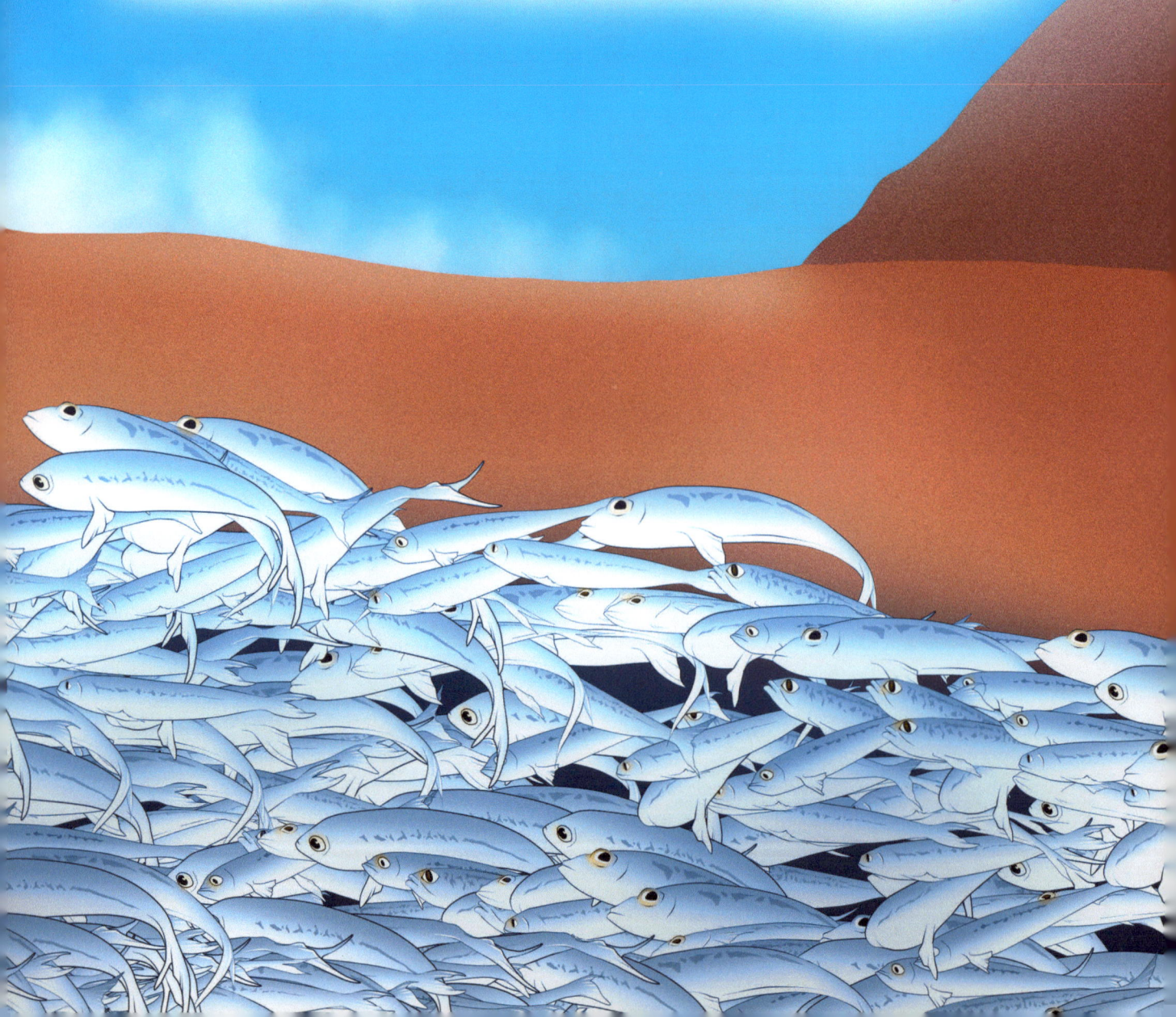

Grandma Margie: **22** is for Twenty-Two Feet Tall, the estimated height of the giant Goliath. In the story of David and Goliath, David, a young shepherd boy, defeated the mighty warrior Goliath with just a sling and a stone.

Zion: Grandma, what were the ten plagues?

Grandma Margie: **23** is for Twenty-Three Plague-Free Days for the Israelites. In Exodus, God sent ten plagues upon Egypt to persuade Pharaoh to release the Israelites from slavery.
The Israelites were unaffected by these plagues.

Zipporah: Grandma, how many animals were on Noah's Ark?

Grandma Margie: **24** is for Twenty-Four Thousand Animals on Noah's Ark. According to the Bible, Noah took pairs of every kind of animal on the ark, along with his family, to survive the great flood.

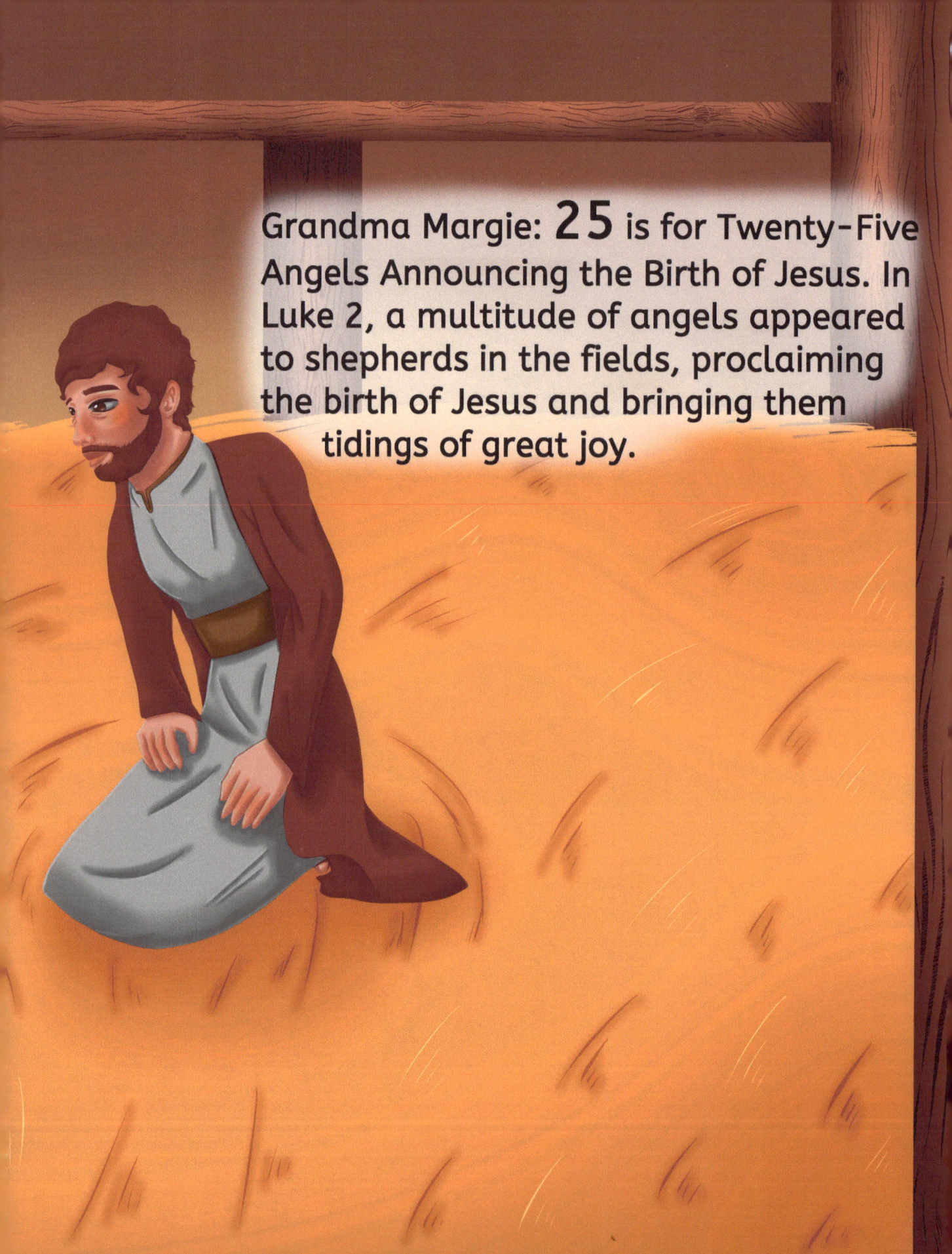

Grandma Margie: **25** is for Twenty-Five Angels Announcing the Birth of Jesus. In Luke 2, a multitude of angels appeared to shepherds in the fields, proclaiming the birth of Jesus and bringing them tidings of great joy.

Zion: Grandma, why was the tomb empty?

Grandma Margie: **26** is for Twenty-Six Disciples Witnessing the Risen Jesus. After Jesus' crucifixion and burial, He rose from the dead on the third day. He appeared to His disciples and many others, proving His resurrection.

Grandma Margie: **27** is for Twenty-Seven Words in the Ten Commandments. God gave Moses the Ten Commandments on Mount Sinai, and they contain a total of twenty-seven words in the original Hebrew text.

Zipporah: Grandma, why did the Samaritan help the wounded man?

Grandma Margie: **28** is for Twenty-Eight Generations in Jesus' Genealogy. In Matthew 1, the genealogy of Jesus is traced back through twenty-eight generations, highlighting His lineage from King David.

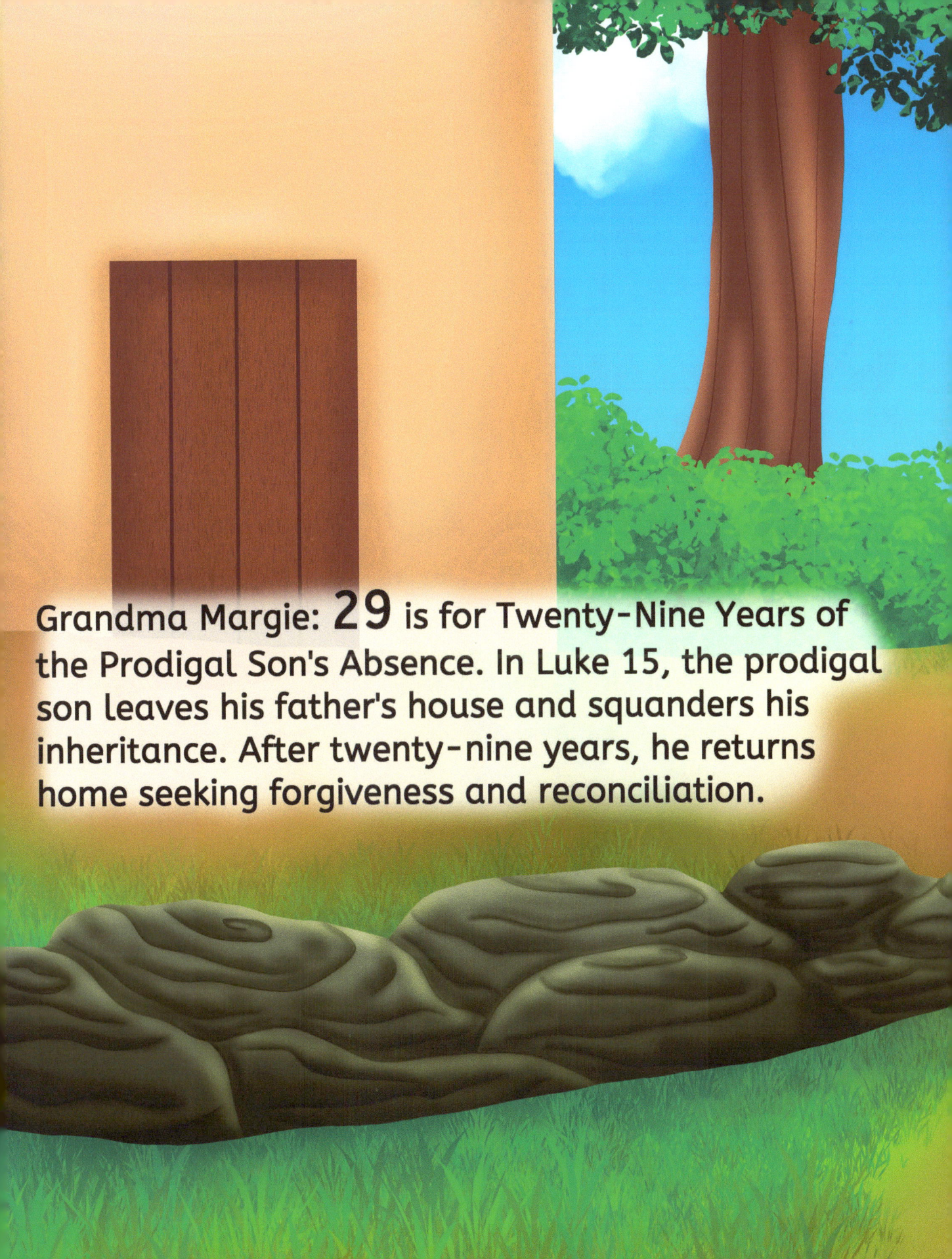

Grandma Margie: **29** is for Twenty-Nine Years of the Prodigal Son's Absence. In Luke 15, the prodigal son leaves his father's house and squanders his inheritance. After twenty-nine years, he returns home seeking forgiveness and reconciliation.

Zion: Grandma, why did Jesus have to die on the cross?

Grandma Margie: 30 is for Thirty Pieces of Silver, the price for which Jesus was betrayed by Judas Iscariot. Jesus willingly sacrificed Himself on the cross to redeem all of humanity from sin and offer eternal salvation. His death on the cross was a demonstration of God's great love for us.

Zion: Thank you, Grandma, for sharing these stories with me and teaching me about the numbers in the Bible.

Grandma Margie: You're welcome, my dear.
It's important to understand the significance of these numbers and how they connect to the stories of faith. Remember, there are many more stories and lessons waiting for you to discover. Keep exploring and learning, and may your faith continue to grow.

Author's Note

Dear Readers,

Creating " Grandma Margie's Tale of the 123's of the Bible: True or False " has been a journey of love and faith for me. My aim was to create a book that would not only entertain but also educate and inspire our young ones. I wanted to introduce children to the beautiful stories and teachings of the Bible in a way that was engaging, accessible, and fun.

The character of Grandma Margie was inspired by my own grandmother, who was a beacon of love, wisdom, and faith in my life. Just like Grandma Margie, she had a knack for making complex ideas simple and relatable. I hope that through Grandma Margie, your children will feel the same warmth and guidance that I felt growing up. Each number in this book represents a significant biblical story or character, carefully chosen to impart important lessons of faith, love, friendship, and servanthood. My hope is that these stories will spark curiosity in your children and encourage them to explore the Bible further.

I believe that learning should be a joyful experience. Therefore, I've incorporated vibrant illustrations and interactive dialogues to make the learning process more engaging. I hope that as your children journey through the pages of this book, they will not only learn the 1 2 3's of the Bible but also develop a love for reading and learning.

Thank you for allowing Grandma Margie and her stories into your home. I pray that this book will be a blessing to you and your children, nurturing their faith and filling their hearts with love and joy.

With love and blessings,

Dr. K.T. Zulkowski